KNIGHTS

Philip Steele

KING*f*ISHER

NEW YORK

Editor: Catherine Headlam
Design: Roger Hutchins and
 Terry Woodley
Cover design: Ch'en Ling
Cover illustration: Christian Hook
Art editor: Ch'en Ling
Picture research: Veneta Bullen

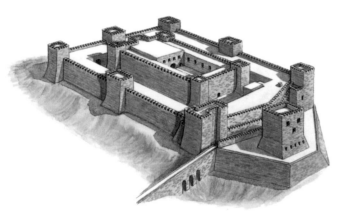

KINGFISHER
Larousse Kingfisher Chambers Inc.
95 Madison Avenue
New York, New York 10016

First published in 1998
10 9 8 7 6 5 4 3 2
2(TR)/0299/VAL/PW(PW)/150R4S
Copyright © Kingfisher Publications Plc 1998

LIBRARY OF CONGRESS CATALOGING-IN-PUBLICATION DATA
Steele, Philip.
    Knights / Philip Steele. —1st ed.
        p. cm.
    Includes index.
    Summary: Tells about the lives of knights throughout history
while focusing on those of medieval times.
        1. Knights and knighthood—Juvenile literature. 2. Civilization,
Medieval—Juvenile literature. [1. Knights and knighthood.
2. Civilization, Medieval.] I. Title.
CR4513.S74 1998
940.1'0088'355—dc21   97-47592 CIP AC

ISBN 0-7534-5154-9
Printed in Italy

CONTENTS

The first knights

Soldiers had fought on horseback throughout the early Middle Ages, but it was only after the 800s that mounted troops started to be seen as a special or elite force. They were now the key to their lords' struggles for power.

▼ At dawn, over 900 years ago, Norman ships were run onto a shelving beach. Men waded through the waves with supplies and led kicking and whinnying horses ashore. The knights' forces might be attacked at any time, so they quickly checked their weapons and their long, kite-shaped shields.

The Normans were descended from Vikings, fierce Scandinavian warriors who had been granted a large area of northern France in 911. Normans went on to seize many other parts of Europe, invading England in 1066 and Sicily in 1072. Their knights were tough, adventurous, and often brutal.

Stirrups

Mounted warriors became a deadly force because of the stirrup, a Chinese invention that reached Europe in the 700s. These supported the rider's legs, steadying him so he could strike with greater force.

▲ The Bayeux Tapestry is a long embroidered panel showing scenes from the Norman invasion of England in 1066. The Norman Duke William conquered the country and became king. He rewarded his loyal knights by giving them large areas of land, so many of them settled in England.

THE AGE OF KNIGHTHOOD

Imagine traveling back to Europe in the Middle Ages. Two great armies are facing each other. A warrior covered in shining armor grips his sword as his warhorse stamps the ground. Suddenly, a shout goes up and the knights begin their charge.... In English, the word "knight" originally meant "servant," but in most other languages, it meant "horseman." Knights were in fact soldiers who swore loyalty to their lord or king. However, they were far from lowly servants. Over the years, knights became powerful and highly respected.

stirrup

The medieval world

The society that the knight lived in was very different from our own. At the top of every country was a duke, prince, king, or emperor. People believed that he alone had a God-given right to rule. The ruler gave land and privileges to the great lords of the country, if they promised to support him and fight for him when necessary. A knight would promise to fight for one of these lords in return for his protection and some land.

▲ A person who held land belonging to someone else was called a vassal. He had to swear loyalty to his lord. The social system depended on oaths of allegiance. Here, Jean de Sainte-Marie swears loyalty to King René of France.

► A knight looks on as fresh horses are brought from the castle to his party. Other travelers on the road have joined his family to take advantage of his protection. They include a priest and a monk, as well as a pilgrim and a lawyer.

A life of toil

Poor people, called serfs, had few rights. They had to work the land and were not allowed to leave their village. Their crops fed the lord in his castle, as well as their own families, and in return the lord was supposed to protect them.

▶ Strong fortresses were needed to protect a knight's land and the people who worked it. After the 1100s, stone walls increasingly replaced wooden ones. These were reminders of the power of kings, lords, and knights.

◀ Poor people spent all their lives working to produce food. But in 1348, many people in Europe died of a terrible plague called the Black Death. Because there were fewer workers, people could bargain for higher wages.

▲ The poor had no opportunities and just tried to survive. But as the Middle Ages continued, some people improved their lives through education or by learning a trade. These people, who included lawyers and merchants, could afford to travel on business, or even go on a pilgrimage—the closest thing the Middle Ages had to a vacation.

If a king ruled unfairly, a powerful lord could claim the throne. In turn, a knight was under no obligation to a lord who broke faith with him.

This social organization, the "feudal system," began to break down during the Middle Ages. It had been based on land, but money was becoming more important. Kings needed money to fight wars. They borrowed it from bankers, who soon became richer than kings.

Crisis in Christendom

During the Middle Ages, Europe was made up of many small kingdoms, principalities, and dukedoms, all jostling for power. English kings ruled large areas of France. German emperors spent as much time in their Italian lands as at home. The Byzantine Empire stretched from what is now western Turkey into Greece.

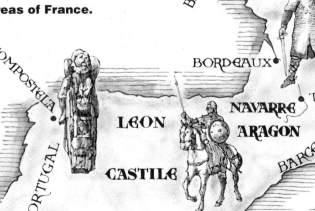

▲ In 1095, Pope Urban II preached to crowds in Clermont, France. He called for knights all over Christendom to launch a holy war, or Crusade, against the Saracens.

▼ Muslim Arabs had conquered all of North Africa by 705. The first Muslim attack on Spain in 711 was followed by two further waves of Moorish invasion, in 1087 and again in 1147. The Moors built fine palaces there, and cities such as Córdoba became centers of scholarship where Muslims, Jews, and Christians lived side by side in peace. It took more than 700 years for Christian knights to reconquer all of Spain.

► During the 1100s, the Normans, who had invaded England in 1066, seized new lands in Wales, Scotland, and Ireland. Royal marriages and conquests extended English rule over large areas of France.

► Rome was the center of the Christian faith in western Europe. It was the home of the pope, who was thought to be God's representative on Earth.

SCOTLAND
IRELAND
ENGLAND
WALES
LONDON
CANTERBURY
HAMBURG
DANES
NORMANDY
BRITTANY
PARIS
WORMS
COLOGNE
MAINZ
HOLY ROMAN EMPIRE
GERMANY
AUGSBURG
CLERMONT
BURGUNDY
MILAN
GENOA
BORDEAUX
TOULOUSE
COMPOSTELA
PORTUGAL
LEON
CASTILE
NAVARRE
ARAGON
BARCELONA
CORSICA
FLOREN
ROM
SARDINIA
TOLEDO
VALENCIA
CORDOBA
SEVILLE
GRANADA
ALMORAVIDS
MEDITERRANEAN SEA

Medieval Europe

In 1100, many of today's countries had not yet been formed. People were loyal to their feudal lord instead of a nation.

All these lands were held together by the Christian faith, and so were known as Christendom. Christendom was bordered by peoples of other faiths. Muslim Arabs and Berbers, known as Moors, ruled a large area of Spain as well as North Africa. Their fellow Muslims to the east were known to the Christians as Saracens, and included Arabs, Turks, and Kurds. Fierce warriors from central Asia, known as Tartars or Mongols, attacked eastern Europe.

NOVGOROD

By 1206, a central Asian ruler known as Genghis Khan had united all the Mongolian tribes. Their warriors soon rode west to devastate Russia, Poland, and Hungary.

▼ The city of Jerusalem and the lands around it were holy to Christians, Muslims, and Jews. From 1096 on, this Holy Land was the scene of the Crusades, a series of bloody wars in which Christian knights fought the Saracens for control.

POLAND

PRAGUE

RUS

KIEV

HUNGARY

BELGRADE

ITALY

APULIA

BYZANTINE EMPIRE

BLACK SEA

Constantinople

MEDITERRANEAN SEA

RUM (ICONIUM)

RHODES

CRETE

ANTIOCH

BAGHDAD

SELJUK EMPIRE

CYPRUS

TRIPOLI

DAMASCUS

ACRE

JERUSALEM

► Travel was difficult during the Middle Ages. The fine roads of the Roman Empire fell into ruin. Horses and wagons had to struggle on muddy or dusty tracks. At sea, small ships were at the mercy of storms and pirates.

MALTA

SICILY

ALEXANDRIA

FATIMID CALIPHATE

CAIRO

ARAB — NOMADS

Chivalry

The ideals of chivalry were celebrated in public with splendid ceremonies, colorful banners, and fanfares of trumpets. Dress became more and more elaborate—and impractical to wear. Strict rules governed every detail of a knight's behavior, whether fighting, hunting, dressing, or dining.

▼ Knights and their retainers ride through the streets of a French town. They have been summoned to their lord's court for a wedding celebration. A noblewoman gazes down at the passing group. She is looking forward to the banquets and festivities in the castle. She may be able to arrange a wealthy match for her daughter, or find herself a courtly champion to further her own interests. For occasions such as a major knighting ceremony or a tournament, vassal knights gathered from throughout the lord's lands, and confirmed their homage and loyalty to him. This was a chance to discuss news from the local countryside and abroad, the stores of food and arms, and plans for battles or defense.

THE KNIGHT'S CODE

The first knights were simply soldiers on horseback, but from the 1100s on, they were expected to follow a strict code of honor. Inspired by Christian teachings, knights were supposed to have courteous and gentle manners. They saw themselves as part of a noble, superior class of people. The word "chivalry" (from *cheval*, the French word for horse) came to stand for these ideals. Chivalry did inspire knights, but rarely prevented brutality or treachery.

Courtly love

This shield was made in Flanders in about 1475, for parading at a mock battle or tournament. It shows a knight swearing loyalty to a lady. Women had few rights in the early Middle Ages, but chivalry demanded that noble ladies were honored and protected. This "courtly love" had little to do with real love or marriage. It was a romantic ideal dreamed up by poets in Brittany, southern France, and Moorish Spain.

◄ Child's play was good practice for fighting.

▼ A boy's first horse might be made of wood and have wheels, and his first lance might be a broom handle.

The page

It was best to start learning all the skills of knighthood at an early age. Young boys of seven or so were often sent to another castle as a page, serving the family and learning good manners.

Becoming a knight

To become a knight you had to be a man, though women did sometimes go on Crusades. You were supposed to come from an aristocratic family, although some people lied about their background.

You needed money or land—being a knight was expensive. An ambitious young man would try to marry into a noble family in order to gain wealth and status. Finally, you had to prove yourself in battle.

spur

sword

▲ The growing page learned how to ride skillfully. He then learned to charge at a quintain, a wooden target that was sometimes designed to swing around and knock him down if he was slow and clumsy.

As a sign of becoming a knight, another knight would tap you on both shoulders with a sword (or cuff you on the side of the head, in the early days). To celebrate Whitsun in 1306, King Edward I of England held a Feast of the Swans at Westminster. The king knighted his eldest son, who then knighted about 300 other young noblemen.

The Maid of Orléans

Although women could not become knights, in 1429 a simple country girl did join the French in besieged Orléans and then led the attack on Paris, dressed in armor. Joan of Arc had heard the voices of saints, telling her to save France from the English. She inspired the French knights but was later captured and burned as a witch.

▼ **In the yard of the castle, a soldier taught the young boys to fight, using wooden or blunted weapons. They could also stay fit by wrestling and swimming.**

The squire

At about 14 years old, the page became a squire. His job was to help a knight prepare for battle and to fight at his side.

The knight

After about four years of experiencing warfare, the squire could become a new knight and be "dubbed." Often the squire would undergo a vigil, a night of prayer, before the ceremony. Swords and gilt spurs were symbols of knighthood that the new knight could now wear.

◀ A Teutonic Knight stands watch over the Order's lands on the Vistula River. In the 1200s, the Teutonic Order, veterans of the Crusades, joined with the Knights of the Sword of Livonia to fight in central and eastern Europe.

Knightly orders

Knights who were fighting holy wars sometimes formed special groups. These were based on the orders of monks, and their members took religious vows. The three most famous orders grew up during the Crusades in the Holy Land. The Knights of St. John were founded in 1099. The Knights Templar were founded in 1119. The Teutonic Order was founded by German knights in about 1190.

▼ King Philip IV of France wanted the riches of the Knights Templar for himself. He accused them of witchcraft and black magic, and from 1307 to 1314 he had them arrested, tortured, and killed. In 1314, the leader of the Templars, Jacques de Molay, was burned.

All three orders built castles and battled against the Saracens, becoming very powerful and wealthy. Many rulers feared the power of these knightly orders. So they decided to found their own orders of chivalry, such as the Garter in England, and the Annunciata and Golden Fleece orders in France. Membership in these orders gave the knights honor and privilege.

◄ **The Knights Templar were a fighting order from the start, but prayer still played a part in their daily routine. They were based in a wing of the royal palace in Jerusalem, thought to be the site of the Temple of Solomon—hence their name. Most of the knights were French, but they also had branches in Spain and the British Isles.**

▼ **Sweating under his helmet, a Knight of St. John charges out against the Saracens. The Knights of St. John began as a religious order, praying and caring for wounded knights and Christian pilgrims. They were often referred to as "Hospitallers," after their hospital in Jerusalem.**

▼ **Though the main orders of knighthood began in the Holy Land, they later looked for other homes, and their influence spread throughout Europe. Spain also had many orders dedicated to fighting the Moors from North Africa.**

ESTONIA
✠ **Teutonic Knights**
LIVONIA ✠ **Knights of St. John**

ENGLAND
Marienburg
CYPRUS
Antioch
Paris ✠ Württemberg
FRANCE ✠ Vienna
Tripoli
Krak des Chevaliers
Venice
Acre ✠ Safad
Haifa ✠ Belvoir
ARAGON
PORTUGAL
Loarre
Arsuf ✠ Jerusalem
Gaza ✠ Beth Gibelin
Calatrava
ASIA MINOR
MEDITERRANEAN
Bodrum
MALTA
SEA
RHODES
CRETE
The Holy Land (see inset)

✠ **Knights of Calatrava**
✠ **Knights Templar**

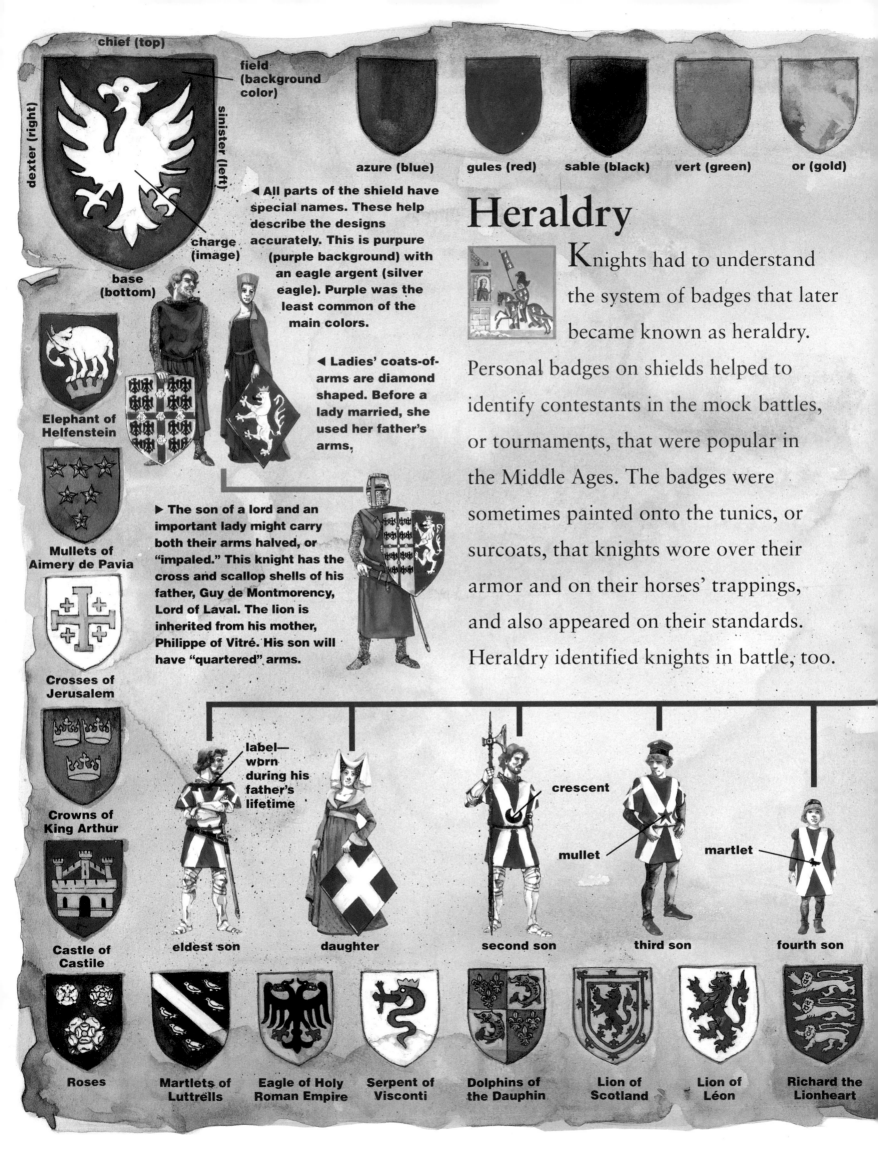

chief (top)

field
(background
color)

dexter (right)

sinister (left)

charge
(image)

base
(bottom)

azure (blue)　　gules (red)　　sable (black)　　vert (green)　　or (gold)

◀ All parts of the shield have
special names. These help
describe the designs
accurately. This is purpure
(purple background) with
an eagle argent (silver
eagle). Purple was the
least common of the
main colors.

◀ Ladies' coats-of-
arms are diamond
shaped. Before a
lady married, she
used her father's
arms.

Heraldry

Knights had to understand
the system of badges that later
became known as heraldry.
Personal badges on shields helped to
identify contestants in the mock battles,
or tournaments, that were popular in
the Middle Ages. The badges were
sometimes painted onto the tunics, or
surcoats, that knights wore over their
armor and on their horses' trappings,
and also appeared on their standards.
Heraldry identified knights in battle, too.

Elephant of
Helfenstein

Mullets of
Aimery de Pavia

▶ The son of a lord and an
important lady might carry
both their arms halved, or
"impaled." This knight has the
cross and scallop shells of his
father, Guy de Montmorency,
Lord of Laval. The lion is
inherited from his mother,
Philippe of Vitré. His son will
have "quartered" arms.

Crosses of
Jerusalem

Crowns of
King Arthur

Castle of
Castile

label—
worn
during his
father's
lifetime

eldest son

daughter

crescent

mullet

second son

third son

martlet

fourth son

Roses　　Martlets of
Luttrells

Eagle of Holy
Roman Empire

Serpent of
Visconti

Dolphins of
the Dauphin

Lion of
Scotland

Lion of
Léon

Richard the
Lionheart

ermine

vair

per pale

per fess

per bend

per chevron

per cross

per saltire

gyronny

E ven today we still use the term "coat-of-arms" to describe a heraldic shield badge. Coats-of-arms were passed down from father to eldest son. They became family badges—a sign of noble birth. They appeared on the seals of documents and can still be seen today in castle halls and on medieval tombs.

The rules of heraldry were laid out in great detail, and each color, pattern, or other design had its own special description, or "blazon," detailed in an old version of the French language.

▲ Five basic colors, or "tinctures," were used in heraldry—blue, red, black, green, and purple—plus two "metals"—gold and silver. There were also patterns based on furs, of which vair and ermine are two. A metal could only be placed on a tincture or vice versa. The "field" could be divided by straight or jagged lines. Standard shield patterns were called "ordinaries." But others had all kinds of charges, or images, such as elephants and roses.

checky

per fess engrailed

▲ In this copy of a medieval manuscript, the Knights of the Holy Ghost are shown boarding a ship for the Crusades.

Their coats-of-arms are displayed on fluttering banners and shields, and on the long pavises that protected them from enemy archers.

per pale nebully

◀ If a coat-of-arms was a badge for the whole family, there still had to be a way of telling its various members apart. Within a family, different children or generations were identified by "marks of difference." The system varied from one country to another. These six people are all children of the English Earl of Westmoreland. Each has his or her own mark.

The herald

The herald was an official serving a king or great lord, who had to know a great deal about coats-of-arms. He also carried messages between warring armies and identified dead knights.

per bend sinister indented

baton sinister —this mark shows that the son is illegitimate

illegitimate son

canton

saltire

cross

pile

chevron

pale

fess

chief

per bend embattled

READY FOR BATTLE

The knight had to make sure that his weapons and armor were kept in good condition. At any time he might receive a summons to war from his lord or from the king. Sometimes it was possible to pay money instead of fighting, but one day he would have to ride to war. He would probably bring along retainers, a small band of local men. These might include his squire, several men-at-arms (mounted soldiers), and foot soldiers or archers. They would join other troops, under the standard of a commander, or knight banneret.

armor mark from Milan

◀ This statue, built in 1480 in Venice, shows an Italian knight named Bartolomeo Colleoni riding to war. He was a condottiere, or mercenary—a knight who was contracted to fight for money rather than feudal duty.

▼ A small armorer's workshop would be crowded with master craftsmen and apprentices learning the trade. Lengths of iron bar were hammered out into sheets and then cut from a pattern with powerful shears. The metal was hammered into shape over anvils and stakes. It could be strengthened by processes of heating and cooling. The finished pieces were then polished and lined with canvas sewn to a leather strip and padded with straw.

Buying armor

If a knight wanted to survive a campaign, he would need to buy a good and often very expensive suit of armor. Low-grade armor was made and repaired all over Europe. But metalwork of the very best quality tended to come from workshops in Italian cities such as Milan and Brescia, or from southern German cities such as Augsburg and Nuremberg, which had access to plentiful supplies of iron ore and charcoal. Rich knights from Britain or France might send an order to one of these centers. Suits could be purchased ready-made, or specially fitted.

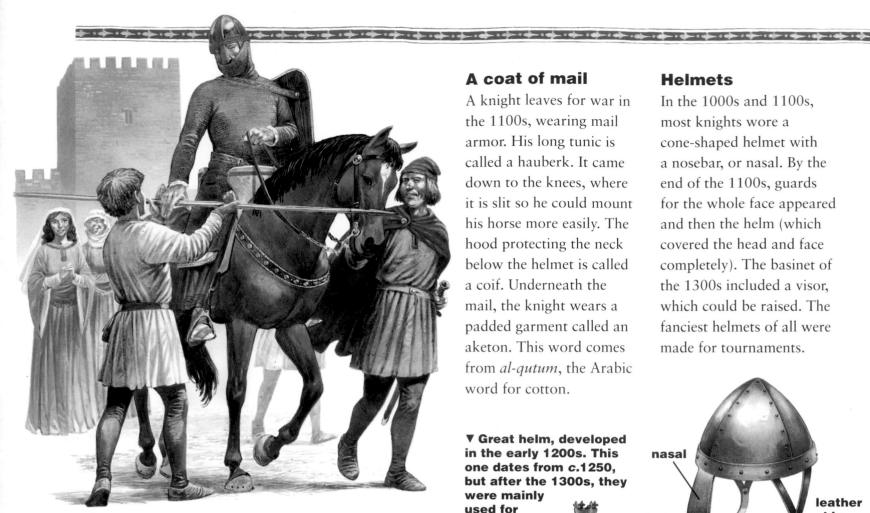

A coat of mail

A knight leaves for war in the 1100s, wearing mail armor. His long tunic is called a hauberk. It came down to the knees, where it is slit so he could mount his horse more easily. The hood protecting the neck below the helmet is called a coif. Underneath the mail, the knight wears a padded garment called an aketon. This word comes from *al-qutum*, the Arabic word for cotton.

Helmets

In the 1000s and 1100s, most knights wore a cone-shaped helmet with a nosebar, or nasal. By the end of the 1100s, guards for the whole face appeared and then the helm (which covered the head and face completely). The basinet of the 1300s included a visor, which could be raised. The fanciest helmets of all were made for tournaments.

Armor

The first medieval knights rode into battle in mail (also known as chain mail). This was a flexible armor that could bend easily because it was made of interlinking iron rings. The armor was shaped so it fitted well, covering the head and forming a heavy tunic over the body. Mail didn't offer complete protection—it could be pierced by arrows. In the late 1200s, knights began to cover their knees with steel plates, and in the next 100 years, more plates were added.

▼ **Great helm, developed in the early 1200s. This one dates from *c.*1250, but after the 1300s, they were mainly used for jousting.**

crest of stuffed leather

nasal

leather chin strap

▲ **Conical helmet, 1000s and early 1100s**

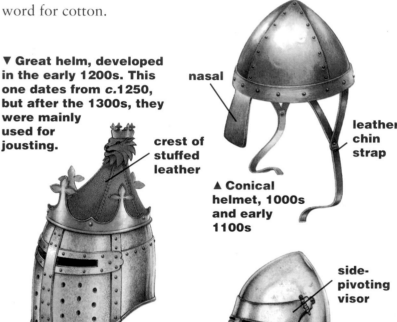

side-pivoting visor

aventail, or removable neck guard

rivets attaching canvas and padded lining

▲ **Basinet from Italy, from late 1300s to early 1400s**

▲ **Barbute from Italy, *c.*1445**

▶ **Gold-etched jousting helmet from northern Italy, *c.*1570**

A trusty shield

The knight's shield protected him from showers of arrows and deadly weapon thrusts. It could also be used to deal heavy blows. The design changed over the years from the long kite shield of the Normans to the smaller triangle shape of the 1300s, made of leather-covered wood. Plate armor made shields unnecessary.

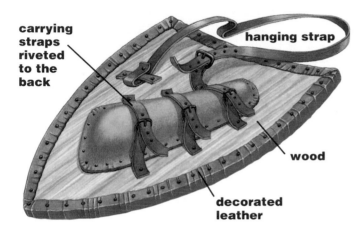

carrying straps riveted to the back

hanging strap

wood

decorated leather

By the 1400s, the knight's body was covered in tough plates of steel. These were well fitted and made of sections joined by rivets and straps of leather. It could not have been easy to fight in plate armor weighing about 50 pounds. However, it was light enough for a knight to move quickly and to get up if he fell from his horse.

▶ A squire removes the plate armor of a wounded knight in the 1400s. This was made of silvery steel. Mail was now worn only as part of the undershirt, or arming doublet, to which the plate was fastened with waxed points, or laces. In the 1500s, new tactics and firearms changed the nature of warfare. Charging knights were less deadly than men with long pikes, and a suit of armor was not much protection against guns.

1 helmet
2 bevor
3 breastplate
4 pauldron
5 besagew
6 vambrace
7 gauntlet
8 cuisse
9 greave
10 sabaton
11 arming doublet
12 waxed points
13 mail gusset

Deadly weapons

The sword, a symbol of knighthood, was cared for and kept close at hand in its scabbard, even during peacetime. King Arthur's legendary sword was called Excalibur, and many knights also gave their sword a special name. A typical European sword of the 1100s had a broad, flat, two-edged slashing blade, with a groove down the center. By the 1300s, the increasing use of plate armor meant that a knight now had to force the blade through chinks and gaps.

Bows and arrows

Powerful crossbows could shoot 600 yards with their bolts, or quarrels, which were short-vaned, iron-tipped darts. Increasingly, a mechanism was used to help wind back the gut bowstring. The longbow was simpler to use, but pulling it needed great strength. It could be shot up to six times per minute (compared to once per minute for the crossbow). The metal-tipped arrows were more than 30 inches long.

goose feather fletchings

longbow

various metal arrowheads

quarrel

crossbow 1400s

gun 1400s

► A knight used a lance for charging into battle. This long wooden spear, tipped with steel, could strike at a distance, knocking the enemy off his horse. Crushing blows could be dealt with an ax, a hammer, or a mace (a kind of club that often had a ridged metal head). The flail was a club that had iron balls attached to a chain. Caltrops were iron spikes thrown to the ground to lame horses and men.

As battle began, the sky darkened with flight after flight of hissing arrows. Horses reared up as enemy soldiers raised pollaxes— blades set on long shafts. One medieval tale, *Song of Roland*, describes weapons being used at close quarters. Skulls crack, brains are splattered, and bodies are hacked to bits. All that counts in battle, says the hero, is iron and steel.

caltrop

dagger 1300s

lance c.1100s

mace 1300s

pollaxe c.1500s

great sword 1400s

sword 1300s

falchion 1200s

flail 1500s

Swords of this period were designed for stabbing and thrusting. The blades became narrower, sharply-pointed, and no longer flat. There were a variety of types to suit the conditions: a dagger or a short sword called a baselard, for stabbing at close quarters; a great sword up to 4 feet long, so heavy that it had to be swung with both hands on the handle; and a broad-bladed, single-edged chopping sword called a falchion.

23

Battling beasts

Horses played an important part in a knight's life. Except for the occasions when he dismounted to fight on foot, the knight's horse really was his key to survival in battle. It brought him into close contact with his enemy, and it allowed him to make his escape. It could even fight for him, rearing up and lashing out with its great hooves.

Carrier pigeons

During the Crusades, Saracen armies used pigeons to carry secret messages from one city or army to another, and the Christians copied them. Pigeons were sometimes killed by trained falcons.

▶ Packhorses were used for carrying an army's baggage. The knight and his men used the best riding horses they could find. The finest warhorses, or destriers, were bigger and stronger.

sumpter (packhorse)

Breeding the best

Mares and stallions of the best quality were set aside for breeding. Their foals were raised and trained for battles and tournaments. The warhorse had to be a stallion—large, powerful, and lively—yet obedient to its master. In battle, a knight and his horse had to act together, perfectly coordinated despite the noise and turmoil around them. The knight's squire led the horse using his right hand, so the animal became known as a *destrier*—the old French word meaning "right-hander." Buying a *destrier* and keeping it groomed and fed was very costly.

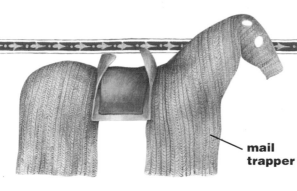

mail trapper

▲ Special armor called a bard was designed for horses. This was originally a covering called a trapper, made of lined cloth or mail.

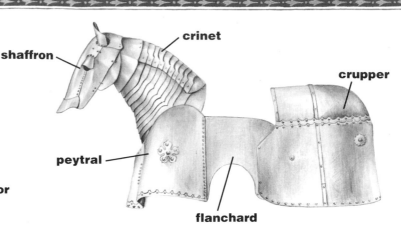

crinet

shaffron

crupper

peytral

flanchard

► Toward the end of the 1400s, Italian knights brought in plate armor for horses, but it was too expensive to be widely used in battle.

hackney or nag (riding horse)

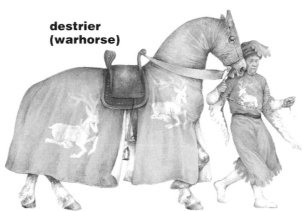

destrier (warhorse)

palfrey (quality riding horse)

The saddle provided the solid platform from which the knight fought. It was often made of beechwood and covered with leather, and had high supports, or bows, at the front and back. The rider's legs were normally stretched out in the stirrups to steady himself, and on his heels he wore spurs, metal spikes to prod the horse into a gallop. By the 1240s, a wheel of spikes called a rowel was sometimes fitted to spurs. The knight carried the reins in his left hand. Perfect control of the horse was needed to stay in formation during the charge.

► This badge shows a Knight Templar giving a lift to his comrade, who rides behind him. The order had humble origins— the two founding knights had only one horse between them.

War dogs

Fierce dogs called mastiffs were bred for keeping watch and guarding supplies in battle camps. Sometimes they were also used to attack the enemy's soldiers.

Open battle

A marching army swarmed over the countryside. The soldiers killed the peasants and burned anything that could be used by the enemy. Some knights rode ahead to find out the enemy's position and strength. Straggling out behind the army were supply wagons, followers, and sick or wounded men. The leaders on each side planned how to trap the enemy, or sometimes how to avoid battle. Bad weather, the lay of the land, the risk of treachery, and hunger all played a part in their decisions.

▲ This is how the fighting groups, or battalions, were drawn up for the Battle of Poitiers, in France, on September 19, 1356. Welsh archers positioned in the woods destroyed the opening charge of French knights.

The remaining French knights joined the battle on foot and were killed in their thousands. The Black Prince then sent a group to attack the French from the rear. Some of the French saved themselves by retreating.

Defenses were hastily prepared by digging in stakes or littering the ground with metal spikes. As the troops were drawn up, they prayed for their lives and shouted support for their side. Battle often opened with a charge by the knights who, with their horses, were targeted mercilessly by the archers. Then hand-to-hand fighting began, creating a hellish nightmare of mud and blood. Knights sometimes fought on foot, forming a dense block of armor and weapons. Battles could last from one to three days, though often the armies were close to each other for several days beforehand.

Life in camp

The army has set up camp, and the hillsides are dotted with fires and the colorful tents of the knights. Common soldiers scour the local countryside for food.

Preparing defenses

The archers hammer pointed stakes into the ground to protect themselves against a charge by the enemy knights. They line up behind the stakes. By this time, the enemy army is very close.

After the battle

Thousands might die in a single battle. Most of the wounded would be put out of their misery by a dagger or sword thrust, but some would crawl off to be bandaged by friends, or monks and nuns.

◄ In 1356, Edward, The Black Prince, raided France with an army of 8,000. Near Poitiers, he was drawn into open battle. Although outnumbered two to one, his army captured the French king and won the battle. The French casualties were several thousand out of 16,000. Of these, 2,426 were nobility—possibly more than the number of nobles captured.

Castles and sieges

Power was held by whoever controlled the castles. There were thousands of castles, all over Europe and the Near East. The first ones built by the Normans were often wooden forts on top of a steep mound of earth. These were gradually replaced by high stone towers, or keeps. Castles became more complex, surrounded by moats, layers of defenses, and massive walls.

In siege warfare, armies would aim to cut off supplies to the castle and starve the enemy into submission. In reply, the defenders would sometimes rush out and attack them. Sieges went on for months as soldiers tried to get through or under the castle walls. More often, they bribed their way in or negotiated terms of surrender.

During a siege, the attackers used force, trickery, or terror to enter the castle. Sometimes they would poison the water in the wells or catapult dead bodies over the castle walls. The defenders shot arrows from slits in the thick walls. They also dropped rocks on the attackers' heads.

▼ Château Gaillard was built in France by Richard I of England. Five years later, in 1203, it was besieged by the French. The defenders starved for six months as the walls were smashed by missiles and undermined by tunnels. In the end, the French climbed up a toilet shaft to break in.

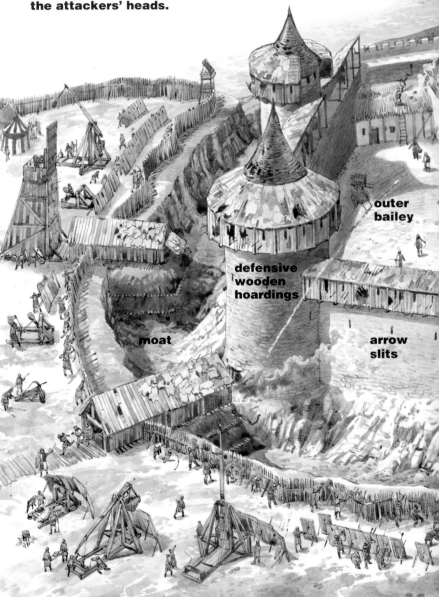

outer bailey

defensive wooden hoardings

moat

arrow slits

Siege weapons

Catapults hurled missiles at the walls. Early cannons, in the 1300s, were poorly made, but as they improved, cannonballs had a devastating effect.

trebuchet (1200s to 1500s): a giant sling with a long arm held down by counterweights, then released, hurling stones from its sling

ballista (1400s): a type of giant bow fixed to a frame, shooting large bolts

mangonel (up to the 1400s): a large catapult powered by twisted cords, shooting stones from its cup

keep

inner bailey

well

battlements

tower

curtain wall

gatehouse

drawbridge

cannon (1300s): a bombard, or mounted gun, firing stone balls

Towers and beams

Towers called belfries, full of soldiers, were wheeled up to the castle walls. Heavy wooden battering rams were swung against the gates to smash them.

belfry (common up to the 1300s)

battering ram (up to the 1400s)

Capture and ransom

During a battle or siege, armies would try to capture as many enemy knights as possible. The prisoners were not normally killed—they were ransomed. This meant that they were held captive until a fee was received. The ransom might be paid by a knight's family or friends. Some ransoms were so high that a knight might remain captive for years— or even for life.

▲ Christians captured in the Crusades are beheaded by the Saracens. During these "holy" wars, both sides tortured and killed large numbers of prisoners of war. When the Crusaders captured Jerusalem in 1099, the streets ran with the blood of the citizens. However, most victors preferred to charge ransom fees.

Knights as equals

One day, two knights would be trying to kill each other in battle. The next, they might be greeting each other politely, according to the rules of chivalry. Often, knights felt that they had more in common with one another than with their own foot soldiers.

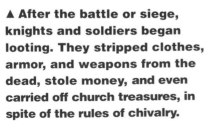

▲ After the battle or siege, knights and soldiers began looting. They stripped clothes, armor, and weapons from the dead, stole money, and even carried off church treasures, in spite of the rules of chivalry.

▶ A captured knight was normally treated well. He might dine with his captors, play chess, or go hunting.

A king's ransom was huge. In 1250, Louis IX of France was captured by Saracens during the Crusades. He agreed to give them the Egyptian city of Damietta and to pay a vast amount of gold. In 1385, English troops hired to fight for King John of Portugal complained bitterly about losing their share of the money when the king did not ransom Castilian captives after the Battle of Aljubarrota. Only knights were worth ransoming. Common soldiers, who had no rich relatives, were simply killed, and the men, women, and children of a captured town were often slaughtered, too.

▲ The payment of ransoms could cause great hardship and bitterness back home. A vassal was expected to sell his land in order to fund his lord's ransom. The people of England paid dearly in taxes when King Richard I, known as The Lionheart, was ransomed in 1193.

Freedom—at a price

The captured knight would probably be held in a castle, supervised by a knight called a constable. At last the money would arrive for his ransom, and his release would be negotiated by a herald. Toward the end of the 1100s, a religious order called the Trinitarians was founded in France. Their aim was to help organize the payment of ransoms for Christian knights captured in the Crusades.

Falconry

During the Middle Ages, European nobility, knights, and ladies all shared a passion with their Moorish and Saracen enemies. It was falconry. Birds of prey such as sparrow hawks, goshawks, and peregrine falcons were carefully trained over many months to catch herons, ducks, pheasants, rabbits, and hares.

▼ The falcon was carried on the hand, which was protected from the talons by a tough leather gauntlet. Leather straps called jesses were attached to a leash to prevent the bird from flying away. The bird was hooded, which kept it calm, until it was released.

Dogs for the hunt

No castle was complete without its kennels, and hunting dogs were well cared for. Spaniels were used for retrieving birds. Greyhounds were bred for their speed for the chase.

Days out

In the fall, with the harvest safely in, knights and their attendants would ride out for a day's hunting. On May Day, nobles welcomed the coming of summer by riding out wearing sprigs of green leaves and flowers. Picnics in good weather were formal affairs, with guests dressed in their most fashionable clothes.

A KNIGHT'S LIFE

 Knights were not always riding off to war. They were also landowners who had to run at least one big estate. They managed large numbers of workers and made sure that farms and mills as well as castles were all kept in good condition. Knights were also expected to carry out all kinds of public duties for the king. They might have to collect local taxes, enforce the law, or act as judges.

falcon

▼ As the king traveled around the countryside, he expected to be put up at the local castle along with all his courtiers, servants, and soldiers.

Some lords and lesser knights may have been eager to impress the royal court, but many must have dreaded the expense and hard work.

The knight's household

Most castles were built for living in as well as for defense. Kings often owned many castles, and lords and other powerful knights might own several, traveling from one to another. Lesser knights often lived in smaller fortified manor houses that were still large enough to include a great hall and often a chapel.

A child's life

Children had chores to help with around the house, and some lessons.

But they would also play with their toys, such as wooden knights operated by strings. Games included hoodman blind, a game of tag like blindman's bluff.

► This is a manor house in England, built in the 1100s but added to over the next 400 years. It is a large country house rather than a castle, but has a moat and is fortified against attacks.

Home comforts

In the early Middle Ages, castles and houses were often cold and damp. Smoky fires burned in the middle of the room, but there were few chimneys. Glass was a luxury—most windows had iron bars and shutters. So letting in light meant letting in the wind. Waste from garderobes, or toilets, dropped into the moat or a cesspit. During the 1400s, life became more comfortable.

Knights shared their busy lives with their families, with pages and squires, soldiers, priests, servants, cooks, and grooms. Much of the management was carried out by the lady of the castle, or châtelaine, especially when the knight was away. Children would have the run of the castle, rushing around the battlements on warm summer evenings, getting in the way of the grooms in the stables, or being chased from the kitchens. In winter, with snow lying on the ground, the children would huddle by the log fire in the drafty solar, or private living room, while their mother embroidered and told them stories.

▼ In northern Italy, noble families often lived in towns rather than in castles. However, they still needed to defend themselves, so they built tall stone towers. San Gimignano, in the Italian region of Tuscany, still has 13 medieval towers. At one time there were 76 of them!

KEY
1 great hall
2 kitchens
3 scullery
4 bedchambers
5 garderobe (toilet)
6 solar (private living room)
7 passage
8 keep
9 stables
10 gatehouse
11 moat

In the great hall

At the beginning of the Middle Ages, chieftains and warlords built large wooden halls, where they lived with their family, retainers, and often their horses and cattle, too. During the 1000s, this "great hall" became one of many rooms, but was still the largest. It was the center of castle life. Here, the household could gather, and the knight could hold important meetings. It also served as the chief dining room, where everybody ate. Visits by the king, a bishop, or a local lord would be marked by a splendid banquet that would often start in the morning and last for several hours.

An aquamanile (for washing hands) in the shape of a knight and a dragon.

Medieval manners

A banquet with important guests was a chance for a knight to show off his polite manners and his hospitality. The meal opened with prayers and with the washing of hands. Strict rules laid out how the pages should serve wine and food to the guests.

Sing for your supper!

Poets and musicians often traveled from one great hall to another. There they sang tales of courtly love and chivalry. If they had any sense, they praised the generosity of their host as well! In southern France they were called troubadours, in northern France trouvères, and in Germany Minnesänger.

The knight, lady, and their guests ate at the high table. The rest of the household ate at long trestle tables. Fine-looking dishes—venison, boar, goose, fish such as carp, enormous pies, and desserts—made a change from the usual broths and stews. Guests ate with their fingers, knives, and spoons. The wealthy dined off gold or silver, but for every day there were plates of wood or pewter, or just thick slices of bread called trenchers.

Favorite hounds chewed on mutton bones on the rushes that covered the floor. After a banquet, the rushes would be swept away and replaced with fresh ones. Around the hall there were chests and hutches for storing tableware.

37

A test of honor

Often at tournaments, the helmets of the competitors were first shown to the ladies of the court. The ladies pointed out if any of the knights concerned had offended against the rules of chivalry—he might have been rude about one of them. If so, the knight could be banned from the festivities.

Grandstands were set up around the grounds, which were decorated with banners and coats-of-arms. The onlooking nobles and retainers became excited, and sometimes violence broke out among the competing groups. So, spectators were searched for concealed weapons before the tournament.

▼ With the development of tournaments, the knights' armor became more decorative. Here, the fancy crests identify the knights.

The tournament

Over 800 years ago, knights began to fight mock battles as a team sport. This gave them a chance to practice fighting and to show off their skills. The first contests were rough free-for-alls, known as melees. Soon all kinds of rules were drawn up. As the idea of chivalry spread around Europe, tournaments became more and more popular.

Jousting

Jousting armor became increasingly specialized, for example, a knight had to crouch forward for the charge in order to see out of the "frog-mouthed" helmet. On impact, he straightened up, and the helmet covered his eyes. The armor's left side was reinforced, since the knights passed left side to left side and received the blows there.

frog-mouthed helmet

tilt

▼ The ladies of court, dressed in their finest clothes, looked on admiringly. A knight would declare himself a favorite lady's champion, wearing her scarf on his sleeve.

Tournaments offered a chance for young knights to make a name for themselves, which could sometimes lead to a profitable marriage. Knights traveled from one country to another in search of glory. The most popular one-to-one fight was the joust, a horseback charge with lances, in which each knight tried to knock the other to the ground. From the 1420s on, the two riders were separated by a fence called a tilt. Prizes such as armor or gold were awarded to the winner.

◄ The tournament was a colorful pageant, but a dangerous one. Although blunted or wooden weapons were introduced, injuries and even deaths were common.

A religious life?

During the Middle Ages, the peoples of Europe, whether Christians, Muslims, or Jews, mostly held simple yet very deep beliefs. They lived in fear of death, whether from starvation, plague, or war. Christians had few doubts about the burning fires of hell or the joys of heaven. They believed that God would punish them for sinning during their life by sending them to hell when they died. Pilgrimage and good deeds would balance out sins they had committed.

◄ By the 1100s, about 500,000 Christian pilgrims each year, including many knights, were visiting Santiago de Compostela, in northern Spain, to honor St. James. This was the third most holy Christian shrine, after Jerusalem and Rome.

Compostela

Canterbury

St. Catherine's, Sinai

Holy badges

Pilgrims who had been to Compostela wore a scallop shell on their hat or cloak, as the badge of St. James. Others wore badges or carried cards to show they had been to one of the many other holy sites and shrines of Christendom. On the way, rogues would often try to sell pilgrims fake relics— pretending they were a part of the holy cross, or a saint's bone.

▲ Pilgrims traveled right across Christendom by ship, on foot, by horse, or by mule to visit one of the many pilgrimage centers. On the route were special inns where they could stay the night.

Christian beliefs guided a knight's life—some medieval pictures even showed Christ himself dressed as a knight. For example, the vigil before a youth became a knight was given over to prayer. When they were old, some knights became monks and prayed forgiveness for their sins—and their sins were many. Knights often killed, tortured, and stole, all in the name of God. However much knights claimed to defend Christianity, in practice, they often fought for rulers who were in dispute with the Church over land, money, and power.

▲ In 1170, four knights burst into Canterbury Cathedral, in England, and murdered archbishop Thomas à Becket, who had quarreled with King Henry II about the powers of the Church. Becket's tomb became a place of pilgrimage.

▲ This stained glass window shows a knight at prayer. Every castle and manor house had its own chapel, and prayer was part of the day. For the many orders of knights who based their lives on those of monks, there could be up to eight prayer services daily.

Death of a knight

This tomb in Salamanca Cathedral, in Spain, belongs to Gutierre de Monroy and his wife Costanza de Anaya.

All over Europe, the tombs of knights and their families can still be seen in churches, chapels, and cathedrals. Many knights paid for church services to be held for their souls each year after they died.

The Moors, whose territory included North Africa, called their land in Spain *al-Andalus*. This was divided into *taifas*, or kingdoms. The reconquest of Spain by Christians began in the north in 727. Wars raged across Spain like wildfire during this time. They were not just simple conflicts between the Christian knights and the Moors. Moorish rulers fought among themselves, and so did the Christian kings. The Christian knight El Cid was respected by both sides, and in 1081 he was hired to defend the Muslim kingdom of Saragossa.

▲ El Cid and his victorious knights took Valencia from the Moors in 1094, after many months' siege. El Cid became ruler of Valencia and the most famous knight in Spanish history. His nickname was taken from the Arabic *al-Sayyid*, meaning "lord." His real name was Rodrigo Díaz de Vivar.

FIELDS OF CONFLICT

Visitors come from all over the world to admire Europe's medieval towns—the narrow streets and the crooked houses, the impressive castles, and the soaring spires of cathedrals. They easily forget that although life in the Middle Ages was often colorful and exciting, it could also be short and wretched. Many parts of Europe and southwestern Asia became killing fields, torn apart by warfare for hundreds of years.

▲ The walls of the Alhambra tower above the city of Granada in Spain. This site includes a massive fortress, the Alcazaba, as well as a beautiful palace, the Casa Real.

The Alhambra was built during the Middle Ages by Granada's Muslim rulers. When it was captured by the Christians in 1492, it marked the end of centuries of warfare with the Moors in Spain.

Holy wars

 From 1096, wave after wave of Christian Crusaders invaded the Holy Land of the Bible, then in Muslim hands. They were encouraged by popes and kings eager for new land and wealth. The Crusaders came from all over Europe, but in the east they were all known as "Franks." Most Crusaders were knights and soldiers, but ordinary people also set out hoping to gain God's approval. Many of them robbed and looted on the way, or were themselves killed.

Warriors of Islam

Saracen cavalryman

Like the Christian knights, many Saracen troops wore mail coats, or hauberks, as armor under their robes. Others were protected by quilted tunics or shirts made up of small steel plates. They carried fine swords and round shields. Turkish archers had short, powerful bows and shot arrows as they rode.

Knights of Outremer

The Crusaders captured Jerusalem in 1099. The lands they conquered became new Christian kingdoms, which were known as Outremer (meaning "overseas"). Many of the Christians who settled in these lands soon adopted the ways of the east.

As the Christian forces marched up the valley toward the waters of Lake Tiberias, they were hemmed in by Saladin's forces. These forces were in three divisions: Saladin himself; his brother Taqi al Din's troops; and Gökböri's division, all supported by a large number of followers and volunteers.

HATTIN July 4, 1187

Saracen volunteers

Taqi al Din's division

Count Raymond's division charges north to break through the Muslim troops and get to water

King Guy's division moves up under the Horns and tries to make a defensive camp

main Christian forces

Grass fires started by Saracens along the route of the Crusader troops' march

Christian rear

Gökböri's division

The Crusader forces were made up of King Guy of Jerusalem in the center, Count Raymond with the advance party, and the rearguard.

In the end some of the rearguard cavalry escape south past Gökböri's division

MEDITERRANEAN SEA

Damascus

Tyre
Acre   Hattin
Nazareth   Lake Tiberias
        Belvoir

KINGDOM OF JERUSALEM

Jerusalem

The Crusades may have been seen as "holy" wars, but they brought lasting terror and misery to the Near East. There were eight major Crusades from 1096 to 1270. The knights' aims became more and more confused. In 1204, a band of Crusaders even broke away to attack the ancient Christian city of Constantinople. In 1291, Muslims captured the city of Acre, and the Holy Land was lost to the Christians forever.

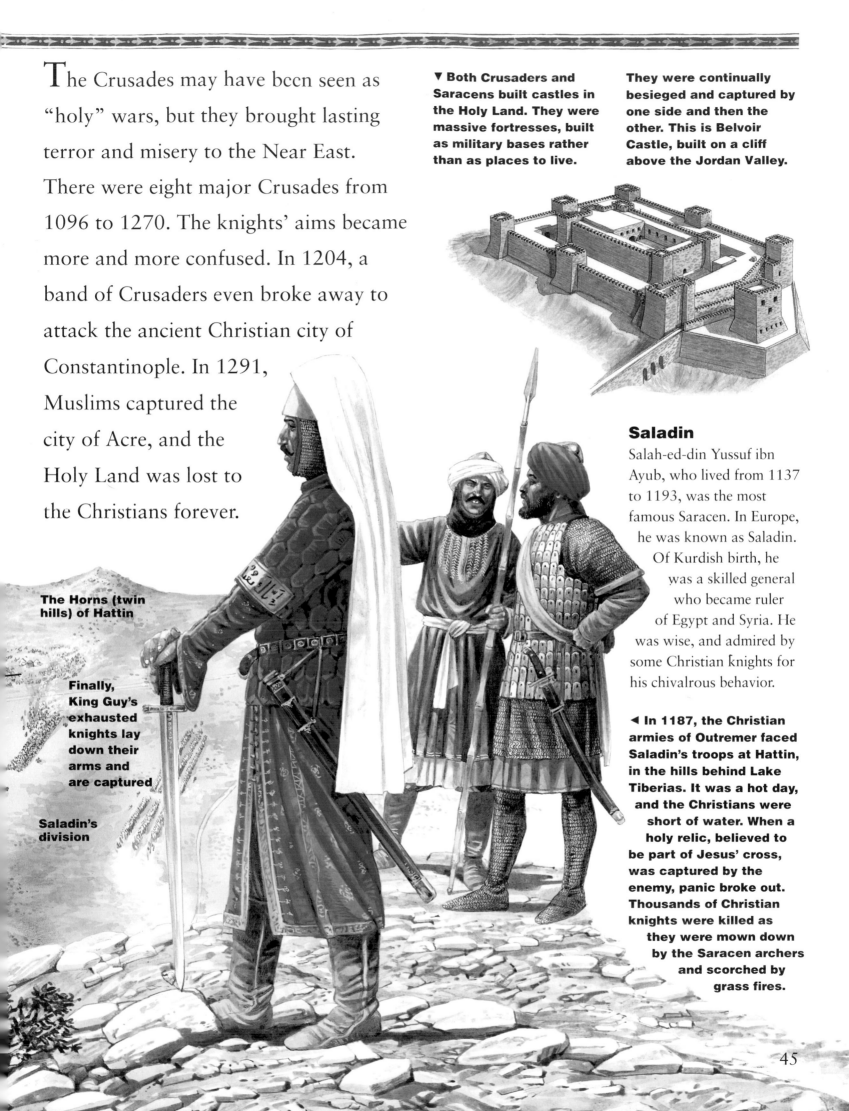

▼ Both Crusaders and Saracens built castles in the Holy Land. They were massive fortresses, built as military bases rather than as places to live.

They were continually besieged and captured by one side and then the other. This is Belvoir Castle, built on a cliff above the Jordan Valley.

The Horns (twin hills) of Hattin

Finally, King Guy's exhausted knights lay down their arms and are captured

Saladin's division

Saladin

Salah-ed-din Yussuf ibn Ayub, who lived from 1137 to 1193, was the most famous Saracen. In Europe, he was known as Saladin. Of Kurdish birth, he was a skilled general who became ruler of Egypt and Syria. He was wise, and admired by some Christian knights for his chivalrous behavior.

◀ In 1187, the Christian armies of Outremer faced Saladin's troops at Hattin, in the hills behind Lake Tiberias. It was a hot day, and the Christians were short of water. When a holy relic, believed to be part of Jesus' cross, was captured by the enemy, panic broke out. Thousands of Christian knights were killed as they were mown down by the Saracen archers and scorched by grass fires.

45

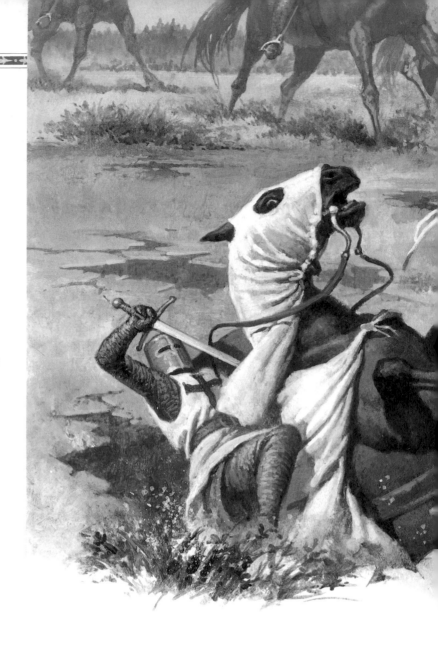

Terrifying Tartars

At St. Mary's Church in Krakow, Poland, a trumpeter still plays once an hour in honor of the city's watchman, killed by a Tartar arrow. From 1237 to 1242, the Tartar armies, made up of Mongols and other central Asian peoples, swept through Russia, Ukraine, Poland, and Hungary. Tartars were cruel soldiers and brilliant horsemen—feared wherever they rode.

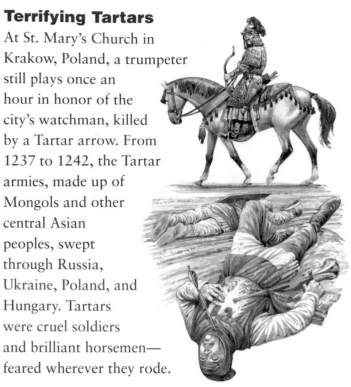

Riding east

Between 1150 and 1250, huge numbers of poor farmers and their families left the crowded lands of Holland and western Germany. They were seeking a new life in Prussia, Poland, Hungary, and the Baltic lands. Joining them were their protectors, veteran knights of the great crusading orders such as the Teutonic Knights. They had a special mission, supported by the pope in Rome—to bring Christianity to the many non-believers who lived in eastern Europe.

▼ The Teutonic Knights called it Marienburg, while the Poles knew it as Malbork. This huge castle, on the Vistula River near Gdansk, Poland, was begun in 1274. In 1309, it replaced Venice as headquarters of the Teutonic Order. The castle included three massive fortresses and a fine palace for the Grand Master of the Order.

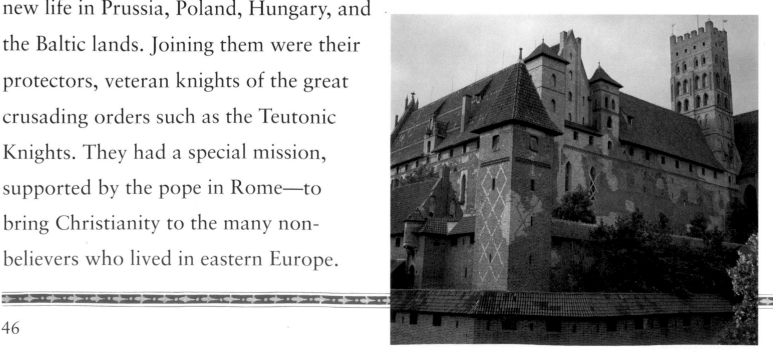

◄ On April 5, 1244, the Teutonic Knights charged across the frozen waters of Lake Peipus, on the eastern borders of Estonia. Their enemies were the Russians of Novgorod, led by Alexander Nevsky. The Battle of the Ice lasted all day. The Teutonic Knights were slaughtered on the ice or drowned in the bitterly cold lake. Their attempt to win land and influence in Russia had been stopped.

The knights had other reasons for riding east besides this holy war. They were keen to defend the rich trading routes set up by the Hansa, a powerful alliance of merchant towns, and to win land and power. All went well, and by the mid-1300s, the Teutonic Order ruled a vast area of land around the Baltic Sea. However, in 1386 the kingdom of Poland united with Lithuania to the north and began to fight to reduce the power of the mighty Teutonic Order.

▼ On July 15, 1410, the knights of Poland, under King Wladislaw Jagiello, fought the Teutonic Order at Tannenberg, in Prussia. The Poles had originally invited the Teutonic Knights east to fight against the pagans. However, over the years, the Poles had come to fear the Order, as it grew ever more powerful. At Tannenberg, the Poles crushed the Teutonic Knights, killing over 200 of them, including the Grand Master Ulrich von Jungingen.

▼ In September 1415, an English army led by King Henry V landed near Harfleur in France. About 1,200 men stayed in the captured town, while 6,000 set out on a march to Calais. It was raining, and conditions were bad. A French army was assembled to get rid of the raiders, and the two forces met at Agincourt.

Killing fields

French was the international language of chivalry, courtly love, and heraldry. France itself was fought over for centuries. Large areas of southwestern France were ruled by the English kings, who held land as Counts of Anjou. Although they were descended from Normans and spoke French, the English kings were at war with France until the end of the Hundred Years' War, a series of battles from 1338 to 1453. Year after year, soldiers from England crossed the English Channel to ravage France.

▼ In 1358, two French knights, the Captal de Buch and the Count of Foix, were returning home from the wars in eastern Europe. Nearing Meaux, they heard that a jacquerie, or peasants' revolt, was in progress.

They entered the town with 25 other knights and their retainers, and slaughtered thousands of poorly armed rebels.

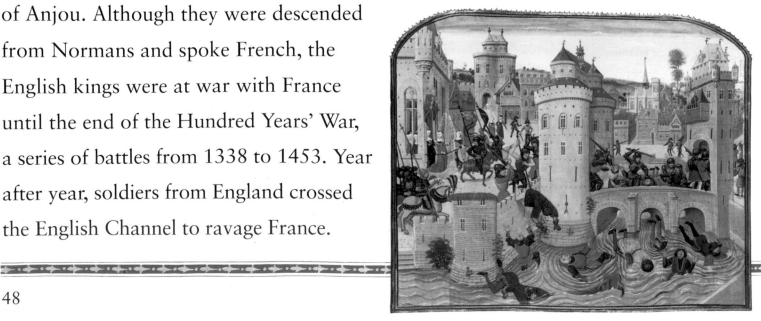

The English weren't the only problem. The state of Brittany was sometimes an ally of France and sometimes an enemy. In the 1300s and 1400s, eastern France, Luxembourg, and Flanders all fell within the grasp of the Dukes of Burgundy. They had a deadly quarrel with the French kings, their close relatives, and fielded large armies which sometimes sided with England against the French.

Carcassonne

Burn the heretics!

In 1208, Pope Innocent III called for a new Crusade—not against Muslims, but against fellow Christians living in southern France. The Cathars followed beliefs that were different from those of the Church, so they were considered sinful heretics. French knights in the north, eager for the spoils of war, hurried south. Thousands of Cathars were murdered. At the walled stronghold of Carcassonne, many of them were captured and burned alive.

Agincourt

On October 25, 1415, French knights tried to block the English raiders in a muddy field outside the village of Agincourt. They failed, and over 7,000 French troops were killed.

END OF AN AGE

About 500 years ago, knighthood was as popular as ever. Tournaments were in fashion, and coats-of-arms were worn proudly. In battle, though, knights were powerless against cannons. Castles lay in ruins. More and more people worked for wages rather than as a feudal duty. States such as Spain, Portugal, England, and France were ready to explore Asia and the New World of the Americas. Western Europe was about to be torn apart by wars between the Church in Rome and the Protestants, who followed the teachings of a monk called Martin Luther. The age of knights was fading away.

Spanish conquistadors in the New World

▼ Constantinople is the city where Europe meets Asia. The city's fall to the forces of the Ottoman Empire in 1453 put an end to the crusading ideals of knighthood.

Constantinople falls

On May 29, 1453, Muslim Turks entered Constantinople after a 52-day siege. This ancient city, known today as Istanbul, was the capital of the Christian Byzantine Empire. It had been founded by the ancient Romans in A.D. 330. The fall of the city was a blow to Christendom and marked the last chapter of the Crusades.

▼ In the late afternoon of May 28, 1453, an eerie hush hung over the city of Constantinople. Suddenly, trumpets brayed and cymbals crashed. A vast army commanded by the Turkish sultan, Mehmed II, stood shouting before the walls of the city.

As sunset approached, the archers on both sides exchanged deadly fire. Soon massive cannons were pounding the walls. Wave after wave of Turkish troops swarmed to the attack. The last Byzantine emperor, Constantine XI, died fighting.

The Christians dropped rocks over the walls and killed the enemy by the thousands, but the Turks kept on coming. At dawn on the 29th of May, the Turks marched in and raised their flags. Thousands of citizens were killed or sold into slavery.

▲ This medieval French illustration shows the death of Roland, one of the finest knights at the court of Emperor Charlemagne. The story of his fatal ambush in 778 was carried on into the age of chivalry.

Tales of chivalry

The battles of the Middle Ages were mostly scenes of horror and misery, but we still tend to think of knights as heroes in shining armor. Like the real knights, we have been enchanted by tales of chivalry, honor, and bravery. The stories of their day told of magic quests, tournaments, and castles. Many of these were old tales rewritten in the language of chivalry.

Medieval stories

The Middle Ages were a time when many old stories and poems were being written down for the first time. Many of them were tales that had been passed down by word of mouth for a thousand years or more. In the medieval versions, warriors and warlords were turned into chivalrous knights and kings, and pagan magic was converted into Christian miracles.

◄ Is this the Round Table of King Arthur's knights? No, it is a medieval fake, originally from the 1300s, and redone in the 1480s and 1800s. It is now in Winchester, England.

▲ In this Victorian painting from 1862, Sir Bedivere looks after the dying King Arthur. The real Arthur was probably a Celtic leader in the 500s. Medieval writers turned him into a brave king attended by knights.

► This picture shows noblemen staging a tournament—in 1839! At this time the Middle Ages came back into fashion. Painters sold pictures of knights and ladies. Some wealthy people even built fake castles to live in.

The tales go on...

Stories of Arthur and his knights started in Wales and Cornwall, and spread to Brittany. Minstrels took them on to Italy and Germany. Around 1470, a knight called Sir Thomas Malory wrote *Le Morte d'Arthur* (from the French, "death of Arthur"). This inspired the poetry of Alfred, Lord Tennyson, in the middle of the 1800s.

▲ In the *Song of the Nibelungs*, written in Germany about 800 years ago, ancient tales about a magical hero called Siegfried were mixed up with historical characters such as Attila the Hun. The old myths of the gods of the Germanic lands became a story of knighthood and chivalry, which, in the middle of the 1800s, inspired four operas by Richard Wagner—the famous Ring Cycle.

▲ *Camelot* was a musical made into a film in 1967. It took its title from the court of King Arthur. The film was based on *The Once and Future King*, a series of stories by T. H. White.

▲ *Ivanhoe* was a very popular novel written by Sir Walter Scott and published in 1819. It was a tale of tournaments, Crusades, and sieges. In the 1950s, it was made into a film (above) and a television series.

► The legendary battles of English outlaw Robin Hood against the evil knights of the Sheriff of Nottingham have inspired countless books and films, such as *Robin Hood, Prince of Thieves* (1991).

Strangely, just as the real age of knights was passing away, people became more and more interested in tournaments and chivalrous stories. Jousts were still popular in the 1600s and again in the 1800s. Even today, books, plays, films, television shows, and computer games return time after time to the subject of knights and chivalry—even if some of the tales are set in other worlds!

▼ Still fighting for truth and justice, Luke Skywalker takes on Darth Vader. The science-fiction film *Star Wars* (1977) is not so different from the old tales of knighthood, even if the swords are now laser-operated. Although it is over 500 years since the Middle Ages drew to a close, the ideals of chivalry have survived.

Other knights

Were there knights in other countries or at other times? There were all kinds of mounted soldiers, but none quite like the knights of medieval Europe. The closest were the samurai of Japan. Between the 900s and 1800s, the samurai lived by a code of honor and ranked high in society. From the 1500s on, they had lofty castles, too. The word *samurai* comes from an old word meaning "someone who serves." Like the European knights, they wore armor, carried swords, and flew battle flags decorated with their lord's badges.

◄ **Samurai, like European knights, were supported in battle by foot soldiers.**

Samurai arms

The classic suit of Japanese armor was called *o-yoroi* or "great armor." It consisted of an iron breastplate, as well as shoulder guards and a skirt of lacquered metal plates. These were threaded together with silk. The samurai warrior was armed with a bow as well as with razor-sharp long and short swords. Samurai fought for warlords and the emperor.

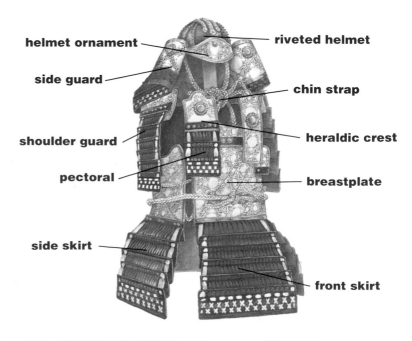

helmet ornament
riveted helmet
side guard
chin strap
shoulder guard
heraldic crest
pectoral
breastplate
side skirt
front skirt

◀ Han warrior 200 B.C.

Horsemen protected Chinese cities from raids by fierce warriors from central Asia.

◀ Roman auxiliary A.D. 200

The Roman army included mounted cavalrymen wearing chain-mail tunics.

▶ Gothic war chief A.D. 400

Fierce warriors from the north and east poured into southern Europe and smashed the Roman Empire.

▶ English harquebusier 1650

This cavalryman from the English Civil War still wears a breastplate and helmet, but carries a gun, the arquebus, as well as his sword.

◀ Prussian officer 1815

At the time of the Battle of Waterloo, the cavalry still fought with lances or swords.

◀ Bengal lancer mid-1800s

Lancers formed an important part of mounted troops in India in the time of the British Empire.

▶ African cavalry 1820

In sub-Saharan Africa, known at the time as the Sudan, Islamic warriors fought with lances against other empires.

▶ Sioux brave 1876

Young Native Americans from the Great Plains formed elite warrior bands, and vowed never to retreat from battle.

◀ French cuirassier 1914

When World War I broke out, cavalry units faced guns and cannons.

▶ In September 1939, Poland was invaded from the west by Nazi Germany and from the east by the Soviet Union. The Polish cavalry rode into action armed with lances, just as their ancestors had at Tannenberg in 1410. However, lances were no defense against the tanks and aircraft of *Blitzkrieg*—"lightning warfare."

Knights and knaves

Alexander Nevsky
(*c*.1218–1263)

Russia's most famous knight, Alexander was the second son of the Grand Duke Yaroslav. In 1240, he defeated the Swedes on the banks of the Neva River and so won the name "Nevsky." In 1242, he defeated the Teutonic Order at Lake Peipus. However, he had to pay tribute to the Tartars, who controlled much of Russia then.

Alexander Nevsky

Bohemund of Taranto
(*c*.1056–1111)

The son of Norman adventurer Robert Guiscard, Bohemund was Count of Apulia in southern Italy. He fought against the Byzantine Empire in the 1080s and joined the First Crusade in 1096, with his cousin or nephew, Tancred. He ended up as Prince of Antioch, in Outremer, and spent three years as a prisoner of the Saracen leader Malik Ghazi before returning victoriously to Antioch.

de Clare, Richard (Strongbow) (*d*.1176)

Strongbow was the son of the first Earl of Pembroke, a part of southern Wales seized by Norman invaders. In 1168, Dermot, King of Leinster, invited Strongbow to support him in his war with another Irish kingdom, Connaught. Strongbow crossed to Ireland in 1170, captured Dublin and Waterford, and married Dermot's daughter. This invasion and marriage marked the start of Norman settlement in Ireland.

Colleoni, Bartolomeo
(1400–1475)

Born near Bergamo, in Italy, Colleoni was typical of his time. As a condottiere, he fought for wages rather than out of loyalty to a lord or state. During the wars between the Italian states of Milan and Venice, he fought for both sides—from 1454 he fought as a commander for Venice, where his statue still stands today.

de Coucy, Enguerrand, seventh Sire (1340–97)

Considered to be the most skillful French knight of his day, Enguerrand was Count of Soissons and Marle. Sent to England as a hostage, he married Isabella, daughter of King Edward III. He decided to remain neutral in the wars between England and France and went to fight in Italy, claiming land ruled by Austria. He was with the French forces defeated by the Turks at Nicopolis in Greece, and died shortly after.

Edward, The Black Prince
(1330–1376)

Named in later years after the black coat-of-arms with three silver ostrich feathers he wore to joust, Edward was the eldest son of Edward III of England. He fought at the Battle of Crécy in 1346 and went on to lead more daring raids into northern France, defeating the French at Poitiers. In 1362, he became Prince of Aquitaine and an ally of Pedro the Cruel, King of Castile and León in Spain.

El Cid (*c*.1034–1099)
Rodrigo, or Ruy, Díaz de Vivar is also known in Spain as Campeador, "the Champion." A knight in the service of King Alfonso VI, he was exiled and took service with the Moors. In 1093, he became a warlord in his own right and in 1094 captured Valencia, which he ruled until his death.

du Guesclin, Bertrand
(*c*.1320–1380)

Born near Dinan in Brittany, du Guesclin was famously ugly. However, he fought valiantly against the English at Rennes, where he was made a knight, and at Dinan and Melun. He also battled at Cocherel with Charles the Bad of Navarre. He became High Constable of France in 1370. Du Guesclin made the French knights more effective as an army, fighting on foot if necessary despite the traditions of chivalry. He paid his troops realistic wages to keep them from looting and killing the peasants, and he encouraged the use of gunpowder. He died during the siege of Châteauneuf-de-Rendon.

Guiscard, Robert (*c*.1015–1085)

This knight was part of the Norman invasion of southern Italy and Sicily by landless knights searching for wealth and territory. He fought the Byzantine Empire as well as the Saracens and championed the cause of the pope against the Roman Emperor, the German Henry IV.

de Hawkwood, Sir John
(*c*.1320–1394)

Having fought at the battles of Crécy and Poitiers, de Hawkwood, born the son of a tanner, was knighted by King Edward III of England. In 1360, he became a mercenary, leading a famous company of English lances that fought for the cities of Pisa and Florence in the Italian wars.

El Cid

John of Bohemia
(1296–1346)

The son of Count Henry III of Luxembourg, John fought for the Bavarians and in Italy, and became King of Bohemia (now part of the Czech Republic). Although he was blinded during a tournament, in 1346 he led 500 knights to Crécy, fighting for King Philip IV of France. Unable to see a thing, John had his knights tie the reins of his horse to theirs and advanced into the thick of the fighting, hacking and slashing with his sword. He was cut to pieces.

John of Gaunt (1340–1399)

The fourth son of King Edward III of England, John became Duke of Lancaster in 1362. In 1372, he claimed the crown of Castile in Spain through his second marriage, but he never gained the country. He did become Duke of Aquitaine, and his descendants (through his third wife) became rulers of England.

le Meingre, Jean, "Boucicaut"
(*c*.1366–1421)

Becoming Marshal of France in 1391, le Meingre was captured by the Turks during an ill-fated Crusade in 1396, in Nicopolis, Greece. He was ransomed, became governor of Genoa, Italy, and was captured by the English at Agincourt in 1415. He died in Yorkshire, still a prisoner of war.

Jean le Meingre

de Montfort, Simon
(*c*.1160–1218)

Of Norman descent, this Earl of Leicester led the cruel Crusade against the Cathars of southern France in 1208. He was killed during the siege of Toulon.

Simon de Montfort

de Montfort, Simon (younger) (*c*.1208–1265)

Son of the above, this Earl of Leicester married the sister of Henry III of England and was sent to govern Gascony (today part of France). He soon fell out with the king and led the English barons in a civil war, setting up the first English parliament. He then quarreled with the barons and was defeated at Evesham in 1265.

Owain Glyndwr (*c*.1354–1416)

This Welsh prince served as squire to the Earl of Arundel, but in 1400 fell into a feudal dispute with his English neighbor, Reginald Grey, Lord of Ruthin. This triggered an uprising that turned into a full-scale Welsh war of independence. Owain gained support in Ireland, Scotland, France, and in England, too. The Welsh were defeated by the end of 1413, but Owain was never captured.

Percy, Sir Henry "Hotspur"
(1364–1403)

The hotheaded son of the Earl of Northumberland, Henry was already fighting at the age of 14. He battled against the French, the Scots, and the Welsh, with whom he later allied himself. He was killed fighting against the king, Henry IV, at the Battle of Shrewsbury.

Richard I of England, The Lionheart (1157–1199)

This king, the son of Henry II and Eleanor of Aquitaine, was a battling knight as much as a ruler, and won great admiration for his part in the Crusades. He had many great victories. However, he failed to take Jerusalem, and made peace with Saladin. Returning home, he was captured by Leopold, Duke of Austria, and handed over to his enemy, the Emperor Henry VI. A very high ransom had to be paid by the English people.

Tancred (1078–1112)

Tancred was of Norman descent, the son of Otho the Good. In 1096, he joined up with his relative Bohemund of Taranto on the First Crusade. He was a skilled soldier, taking part in sieges all over the Holy Land. He ended up as one of the most important rulers in Outremer, governing Tiberias, Antioch, and Edessa.

Tancred

Wallace, or Walays, Sir William
(*c*.1274–1305)

This Scottish knight began Scotland's war of independence against England, defeating Edward I at Stirling Bridge in 1297. Defeated in turn at Falkirk in 1298, he fled to France, but was captured back in Scotland in 1305. He was taken to London where he was hanged and beheaded. Then his body was cut in four and sent to the towns of Perth, Newcastle, Berwick, and Stirling.

Wolfram von Eschenbach
(*c*.1170–1220)

Not all knights were famous for their battles. Von Eschenbach was a minor knight who is best remembered as a poet, or Minnesänger. He was born in Bavaria and joined the court of Hermann of Thuringia at Wartburg Castle. Von Eschenbach wrote one of the great tales of knighthood, *Parzival*.

Knights in fiction

Arthur

The historical Arthur was probably a British Celt of the A.D. 500s. He may have been a general (dux) at the head of a long campaign against the Angles and Saxons who had invaded after the fall of the Roman Empire. His name crops up in early Welsh myths and legends, and by the later Middle Ages, writers had transformed him into a mighty king, and leader of the Knights of the Round Table. Tales of King Arthur's chivalry spread over Europe and have inspired writers ever since.

KING ARTHVR

Bedivere, or Bedwyr

This figure appears in some of the earliest Welsh tales to mention King Arthur. In *Le Morte d'Arthur* by Sir Thomas Malory (*c.*1470), he becomes one of the most important Knights of the Round Table. When Arthur lies dying, it is Bedivere who hurls his sword, Excalibur, into the lake.

Excalibur

The Canterbury Knight

Geoffrey Chaucer (*c.*1343–1400) was an English poet who wrote a series of tales as if they were being swapped by a group of pilgrims on the way to Canterbury. One of Chaucer's pilgrims is a knight, described as being chivalrous and brave. He is a veteran of 15 battles who has fought in wars against Turks and Moors, and yet is always gentle and polite. He has fought in tournaments and owns a fine set of horses. His tunic is stained with the marks of his armor.

Dietrich of Bern

Just as the warrior Arthur reappears in medieval tales as a splendid king, so does Theodoric reappear in German legends as Dietrich of Bern, a chivalrous knight. He features in the *Song of the Nibelungs*, a grim story of honor and revenge written down in Germany in the 1200s. The real Theodoric was a king of the Ostrogoths, who died in 526.

Ector, Sir

According to *Le Morte d'Arthur*, the wizard Merlin placed the baby Arthur in the care of Sir Ector, to conceal from his enemies the fact that the boy was the son of Uther Pendragon. A recent version of the story appears in *The Once and Future King*, four Arthurian tales written by T. H. White in 1958. The first of these tales, *The Sword in the Stone*, was made into a film by Walt Disney.

Falstaff, Sir John

This humorous character was created by the English playwright William Shakespeare in the 1590s, although he may have been based on a real knight, Sir John Oldcastle. Falstaff is old, fat, and jolly. He drinks and boasts a lot, but is really a coward. There were probably many knights like him in real life!

Galahad

The name Galahad appears in later stories about King Arthur. He is the son of Lancelot and the princess Elaine, and is the purest knight of all. He is the only knight to find the Holy Grail. The Grail was believed to be the cup from which Jesus drank at the Last Supper. According to legend, it was brought to the British Isles. In fact, the idea of the Grail probably began with ancient Celtic folktales about a magic cauldron.

SIR GALAHAD

Ganelon

Also known as Gan of Mayence or Gano of Moganza, he was one of Charlemagne's twelve special knights, called paladins. Charlemagne (747–814) was king of the Franks, and a battle against the Moors in Spain gave rise to the heroic tale, *Song of Roland*. In this tale, the paladins are transformed into medieval knights. Ganelon betrays the ideals of chivalry and so brings about the death of Roland (another of the paladins).

Gareth ("Beaumains")

In the legends of King Arthur, Gareth is the son of Arthur's sister and King Lot of Orkney. He arrives unknown at his uncle's court at Camelot, and is put to work in the kitchens. His fine hands are noticed by Kay, who calls him by the French name, *Beaumains*, meaning "beautiful hands."

Gawain

The eldest brother of Gareth, Gawain is described as one of the bravest knights of Arthur's Round Table. In Welsh tales, he was called Gwalchmai, in French, Gauvain. In one story, he goes in search of a strange Green Knight. On the way, his honor is tested in different ways.

Hagen

In the *Song of the Nibelungs*, Hagen is a knight in service to the rulers of Burgundy. He kills the hero Siegfried, whose widow later kills him and his comrades.

Kay, or Cai

This warrior also appears in ancient Welsh tales, where he is linked with Arthur and magical deeds. In later stories from England and France, he is shown as a boastful, hotheaded, clumsy knight, the foster brother and steward of King Arthur.

Lancelot

This Arthurian knight first appears in French versions of the tale. He is the son of King Ban of Benwick, in Brittany, and becomes the most handsome, honorable, and daring Knight of the Round Table. He is the king's best friend, but falls in love with Arthur's wife, Guinevere. In the end, Lancelot becomes a monk, and Guinevere a nun.

Mordred, or Medraut

In some tales, Mordred is the son of Arthur, in others his nephew. It is the evil Mordred who brings the golden age of knighthood to an end. In the last great battle, he is slain by Arthur, but not before wounding the king fatally in return.

Olivier

Also known as Oliver, Oliviero, or Ulivieri, this knight appears in the French *Song of Roland* as a chivalrous and wise knight who becomes firm friends with Roland after they have fought each other.

Palamedes

This is the only non-Christian knight at the court of King Arthur, a noble Saracen.

Perceval of Galles

Known in the original Welsh tales as Peredur and in German romances as Parzival, Perceval's story dates back to ancient times. Later tales describe his search for the Holy Grail.

Don Quixote

This character was invented by the Spanish writer Miguel de Cervantes in the 1600s. He tells the story of a simple man who is so excited by the tales of chivalry that he has himself knighted by an innkeeper, becoming "Don Quixote." This latterday knight lives in a fantasy world, jousting at windmills and fighting armies of sheep, accompanied by his servant Sancho Panza and his horse Rocinante.

Don Quixote

Robin of Locksley

According to some old English folktales, the mythical outlaw and popular hero Robin Hood was actually a knight of the 1100s, born at Locksley in Nottinghamshire. He robbed the rich to provide for the poor. Some stories say he was really Robert, Earl of Huntingdon.

Roland

The heroic knight described in the *Song of Roland* has his origins in history. He was one of the elite paladins of Charlemagne, and died in 778 fighting off a Basque ambush in a mountain pass at Roncesvalles in the Pyrenees. In Italian stories, Roland is called Orlando.

Sheriff of Nottingham

In many folktales the heroes are outlaws fighting against injustice. One of the most famous of these tales is about the English hero Robin Hood. His great enemy is the Sheriff of Nottingham, the evil knight who governs the region around Sherwood Forest while King Richard I is away at the Crusades, though in medieval tales, the king is Edward.

Siegfried

Siegfried was a hero of ancient German myths. In the medieval *Song of the Nibelungs*, he becomes a noble prince of the Rhineland who is murdered by Hagen.

St. George

This Christian saint was originally a Roman soldier who died in A.D. 303. He was believed to have helped the Crusaders in Antioch and was later adopted as the patron saint of England, Aragon, and Portugal. Since the Middle Ages, he has always been shown as a chivalrous knight in armor, killing dragons and rescuing maidens.

St. George

Tristan, or Tristram

This hero is a knight serving King Mark of Cornwall. He is sent to Ireland to get Iseult (also known as Esyllt, or Isolde), who is to be Mark's new bride. On the way back, the couple accidentally drink a potion and fall hopelessly in love. The lovers flee to Brittany where Mark seeks out and fights Tristan, fatally wounding him. The story spread from Cornwall to Brittany, and from there to France and Germany.

Glossary

aketon A padded garment worn underneath mail or as their only defense by some soldiers of lesser rank.

aketon

allegiance The loyalty owed by a vassal to his lord under the feudal system.

armorer A metalworker who specialized in making armor.

banner A rectangular heraldic flag showing a coat-of-arms. Only one was made for each bearer-of-arms.

bard A set of armor designed for a warhorse.

Black Death Various forms of the bubonic plague, a terrible illness that swept through Asia and Europe between the 1330s and 1350s. In places, it killed as many as one person in three.

castle A heavily fortified building, lived in by a whole community of people. Rich knights might have had many castles to defend their lands.

chivalry The ideals of knighthood, by which a knight is generous toward noble enemies and honorable toward women.

Christendom All the lands where people held the Christian faith.

coat-of-arms
The badge of a family or organization, drawn up according to the rules of

coat-of-arms

heraldry. Originally named after the surcoat worn by the knight, the coat-of-arms appeared on shields and banners used in both battle and tournaments.

coif A hood made of mail and worn on the head. The helmet was worn on top of it, leaving the bottom edges of the coif to protect the neck.

condottiere An Italian knight who was contracted to fight for money. The contract, or condotta, was drawn up between the leader of the mercenary band and his employer, and promised to provide a certain number of men for a particular conflict or battle.

constable A knight appointed by the king to hold a castle or take care of royal interests.

courtly love The honoring of a woman by a knight, as idealized by the poets of southern France.

crossbow A very powerful bow. The first ones were stretched by hand, but the later versions used a variety of mechanisms. They shot arrows called bolts or quarrels.

crossbow

Crusade A "holy" war fought by Christians against people with different religious beliefs. These were mostly Muslims and sometimes heretical Christians.

destrier A large warhorse of the best quality.

dub To make someone a knight by placing the flat blade of a sword on his shoulders. In the

early days of knighthood, knights were dubbed with a cuff of the hand.

dukedom A region ruled by a duke. Some dukedoms, such as the Dukedom of Burgundy, were more powerful than small principalities and kingdoms.

falconry The training of birds of prey to hunt.

feudal system A social system common in the early Middle Ages, in which one person was granted land or protection by a lord in return for their services or labor.

great hall The large hall in a castle, often used for dining.

hauberk A long tunic made of mail, used as armor.

herald An official working for a king or noble. He agreed the rules of battle with the enemy and carried messages between parties at war. He also knew all about heraldic devices and after a battle listed the knights who had died.

heraldry The system of signs and family badges used on shields and flags from the Middle Ages onward.

heretic Someone whose religious beliefs are thought to be sinful by religious leaders.

Holy Land The lands in the Middle East that are holy to Christians, Jews, and Muslims.

jousting Combat during a tournament, in which one knight on horseback charges another with a lance.

knight A soldier who, during the Middle Ages, was ranked among the nobility in Europe.

knight banneret A high-ranking knight who rode into battle under his own banner. He would often command several lances.

lance (1) A long spear, almost always carried on horseback. (2) A unit in a medieval army, led by a knight. This would be made up of the knight himself, mounted archers, often another mounted soldier, and a crossbowman and pikeman on foot.

longbow A long and powerful wooden bow that shot arrows. It was popular with archers in the British Isles.

mace A heavy club, normally used by a knight to clobber the enemy.

mail Flexible armor made of interlinking iron rings, also known as chain mail.

mercenary A soldier who hires out his services for money.

mail

melee A free-for-all fight, staged as a competition in a tournament.

Middle Ages A term used by historians to describe the period between the end of the Roman Empire in A.D. 476 and the start of our modern world in about 1500.

Moor One of the peoples of North Africa, especially a Berber or Arab. For more than 500 years, the Moors also lived in Spain.

order A religious organization of monks or knights.

page A young boy who served a noble family as part of his training for knighthood.

pennon A small flag carried on a cavalry lance, including a badge, coat-of-arms, or colors. Pennons were flown by a lord's retainers.

pilgrim A person who travels to a holy shrine or city. Christians went first and foremost to Jerusalem and Rome; Muslims to Mecca.

plate armor Armor made out of sheets of solid metal. This was also known as white armor.

pope The leader of the Roman Catholic Church.

principality A region ruled by a prince.

quintain A target on a post, used for practice with a lance.

ransom The fee paid for the release of a captured knight.

quintain

retainer One of a knight's armed followers. The knight supplied his retainers' horses and weapons.

samurai The Japanese landowning and warrior class that was the nearest equivalent to the knights of medieval Europe.

Saracen The European word for a Muslim warrior, normally an Arab, Turk, or Kurd.

scabbard The sheath or casing for the blade of a sword.

serf Someone who had to work on the land under the feudal system.

siege The cutting off or blockade of a town or castle, in order to starve it, attack it, and make it surrender.

solar The private living room, usually off the great hall, in a medieval castle or manor house.

spur A point or wheel fastened to the heel of a rider, used to make a horse go faster.

squire In the Middle Ages, a youth who was in training for knighthood. He served a knight for several years.

standard A flag flown to mark the rallying point on a battlefield or the headquarters of the bearer of arms. It was normally swallow-tailed.

stirrup A support for the foot when riding horseback.

sumpter A horse or mule used to carry baggage.

tilt (1) A barrier erected between two jousting knights. (2) To joust.

tournament A mock battle, for amusement or training.

trapper A horsecovering made of cloth or mail, used both in battle and in peacetime.

undermine To tunnel underneath a wall to make it collapse.

vassal Anyone who was granted land in return for services by a feudal lord.

vigil

vigil Staying awake, being on watch, or praying all night before being made a knight.

Index

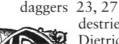

Acknowledgments

The publishers would like to thank the following
illustrators for their contributions to this book:

Julian Baker 5*mr*, 12*ml*, 18*ml*, 20*br*, 21*tl*, 22*br*, 23*b*, 39*tl*, 40*tr*,
45*tr*; **Gino D'Achille** (Artists' Partners) 22–23*t*, 26–27, 46–47;
Peter Dennis (Linda Rogers Associates) 20*tl*, 21*br*, 25*br*,
28–29, 34–35, 36–37, 46*tl*, 47*br*, 49*tr*;
Francesca D'Ottavi 16–17; **Les Edwards** (Arena) 14*l*, 15*tr*,
15*br*, 50–51; **Martin Hargreaves** (Illustration) 18–19;
Christian Hook 40*l*, 55; **Angus McBride** (Linden Artists) 4–5,
12–13, 30–31, 48–49; **Danuta Mayer** 10–11, 38–39, 41*tl*;
Clare Melinsky 56–57, 58–59, 60–61; **Nicki Palin** 6–7,
24–25, 32–33, 34*tr*, 54; **Mark Peppé** (B.L.Kearley Ltd)
7*t*, 22*bl*, 27*r*, 39*tr*, 44*tr*; **Richard Phipps** (Illustration) 8–9;
Clive Spong (Linden Artists)15*tl*, 26*bl*, 40*br*, 42*tl*,
44*bl*, 47*mr*, 48*t*, 50*bl*; **Bob Venables**
(Thorogood Illustration) 42–43

Decorative border and six chapter illuminations
by **Danuta Mayer**

The publishers would also like to thank the following for
supplying photographs for this book:

A.K.G. London: 5*tr*;
Bibliothèque Nationale, Paris: 37*tr*, 52 *tl*;
Board of Trustees of the Royal Armouries: 52*b*;
Bridgeman Art Library: 11*br*, 14*br*, 30*tr*, 36*cl*;
Corbis U.K. Ltd.: 35*br*, 43*br*, 46*br*;
E. T. Archive: 6*tr*, 8*tr*, 13*tr*, 33*br*, 48*bc*;
Fotomas Index: 53*tl*;
Fine Art Photographs: 52*cr*;
Ronald Grant Archive: 53*tr*, 53*c*, *cr*, *br*;
Sonia Halliday: 41*cl*;
Hampshire County Council: 52*cl*;
Peter Newark's Pictures: 17*cr*, 50*cl*;
Popperfoto: 55*br*;
Scala: 18*bl*, 41*br*.